Watching from the Walls

Watching from the Walls

Waiting for Jesus with Hope and Expectation

AN ADVENT STUDY

Andrew C. Thompson

TRINITY BOOKS

WATCHING FROM THE WALLS

COPYRIGHT © 2020 Andrew C. Thompson

Unless otherwise noted, Scripture quotations are from the ESV® Bible (The Holy Bible, English Standard Version®) copyright © 2001 by Crossway, a publishing ministry of Good News Publishers. Used by permission. All rights reserved.

Scripture quotations marked NIV are taken from THE HOLY BIBLE, NEW INTERNATIONAL VERSION® Copyright © 1973, 1984, 2011 by Biblica, Inc.™ Used by permission. All rights reserved worldwide.

Scripture quotations marked KJV are taken from the Holy Bible, King James Version, Cambridge, 1796

Scripture quotations marked NRSV are taken from the Holy Bible: New Revised Standard Version/Division of Christian Education of the National Council of Churches of Christ in the United States of America.–Nashville: Thomas Nelson Publishers, c. 1989. Used by permission. All rights reserved.

ISBN: 978–1-953272-00-3

TRINITY BOOKS
AN IMPRINT OF THE GLOBAL GOSPEL, LLC
P.O. BOX 10556
FAYETTEVILLE, AR 72703

PRINTED IN THE UNITED STATES OF AMERICA

For Alex Jackson

CONTENTS

Acknowledgements

This short little book is the result of long years of reading, teaching, and preaching about the Nativity story of our Lord Jesus Christ. It began twelve years ago with a project in collaboration with a dear friend, Rev. Alex Jackson, who was pastoring a church in Tennessee at the same time I was pastoring a church in North Carolina. We wanted to develop a sermon series together for Advent one year that we would each preach in our own churches. The conversations we had and the stories we shared were both a joy and a help to one another in that process. We hoped our Advent project might turn into a book we would write together, but time and circumstances ultimately got in the way. Nevertheless, my work with Alex led me down a path of thinking and reflecting over the years on how the Old Testament theme of the "watchmen on the walls" was a perfect way to characterize the Christian calling to keep watch each Advent season, both to remember the birth of Jesus and to anticipate his coming return. I'm grateful to Alex for many things, including the way our conversations and collaboration back then have shaped the book that did eventually get written. I have dedicated it to him.

Two congregations I have served have played a role in how the *Watching from the Walls* material has been developed. The first was Mt. Carmel United Methodist Church in Henderson, NC, and the second is my current appointment, First United Methodist Church in Springdale, AR. These two churches are very different in many ways, but what they have in common is that they have nurtured my family and me with great love during the time we have been with them. I'm very grateful to them for that, as I am for their willingness to receive the preaching and teaching material that eventually turned into *Watching from the Walls*. In the case of my current congregation in Springdale, I turned what originated in sermon form into a written Advent study that many individuals and Sunday school classes used recently. That process (and the feedback I received!) allowed me to undertake the final revisions that led to the book in its present form.

This book would also not have been possible without colleagues and friends who played a significant role in its development. I'm thankful on that count to Kristal Williams, Lori Krie, and Joanna Davis (without whom I can't get through a week). I'm also grateful to Dr. Matthew Johnson, who is both a friend and a colleague in ministry. My work with him on this book has been a true joy, and it holds out the hope of many future shared endeavors in the years to come.

Finally, I am thankful to my family, my wife Emily and our children Alice, Stuart, and Anna Charlotte. They indulge my pastoral schedule and my reading habits with greater patience than I deserve. I only hope that I am the kind of husband and father that they deserve more days than not.

All thanks I offer ultimately to the one true God—Father, Son, and Holy Spirit. I pray that this study would lead people to know Jesus Christ in the glory of his Incarnate love for each and every one of us.

Introduction
Finding Your Place in God's Story

God's word comes to us in the Bible. The Bible is the book that tells us God's story with his people. And he wants to invite you into that story.

One of the most wonderful things about the Bible is the way that it is both time-bound and eternal. It is time-bound because the people, places, and events that it describes lived and happened at a particular point in history. Yet it is eternal because those same people, places, and events have significance for every era. And since we are a part of God's people even today, that makes God's story in the Bible our story too.

This book is about the part of God's story that focuses on the birth of his Son Jesus Christ into the world. In the Christian year, we usually read about the birth of Jesus during the season of Advent, which includes the four weeks leading up to Christmas. I hope this book can be a helpful way for you to learn about how Jesus came into the world as you get ready for Christmas. On the other hand, there is never a bad time to learn more about Jesus! So you might find it to be a useful resource at any time of the year.

Additionally, one of my greatest hopes in writing this study is that it will do more than just help you learn "about" the story of Jesus. I want it to help you enter into that story. I want you to find your place in it—to come to know it as *your* story, with a role for *you* to play. Part of the Bible's eternal relevance is that it is always present, always new. Its message is not just limited to the time in which it was written down. It has a message to speak here and now, and that message is meant for you. In fact, the Bible wants to draw you into its story so that you can find a place there.

I believe that we can begin to put ourselves in the story of Scripture when we learn how to read it the right way. Let me explain what I mean.

Our six-year old daughter Anna Charlotte loves to pretend. At least once per day, she will spontaneously start skipping and dancing around our living room. She goes in circles, around and around the edge of the room behind the furniture. She'll sing songs or talk softly to herself, and she gets to the point where she's completely oblivious to anyone or anything else around her. If you stop her and ask her what she's pretending, she'll usually tell you that it is a movie or a TV show that she's watched recently. What has always struck me about the way Anna Charlotte pretends is that she makes herself a character in the story that she has in her mind's eye. She *enters in* and becomes a part of it. She isn't just imagining the story in her head. Instead, she's leaping into it as a participant and taking an active role herself.

You know, there is a reason why Jesus tells us that we need to become like little children if we ever want to enter the kingdom of heaven (see Matthew 18:2-3). He wants us to see with fresh eyes, and to hear with new ears. I believe he wants us to see ourselves as having a role to play in his kingdom-building story. The season of Advent is a season of expectant waiting, as we get ready to celebrate anew the birth of our Savior into the world. Our waiting is meant to take on an active character—we are, in the language of the Old Testament, the "watchmen on the walls" who are looking for the coming of our Messiah. So as you begin this journey into the Nativity story, I hope you'll do so as someone who is ready to *read* and *pray* and *participate* in a new way. This is God's story, and it is God's story with us.

That means it is God's story with *you*.

Chapter One
The World Holding Its Breath

Listen! Your watchmen lift up their voices;
   together they shout for joy.
When the Lord returns to Zion,
   they will see it with their own eyes.
      — Isaiah 52:8 (NIV)

What does it mean to *watch*?

We can watch in a lot of different ways. Sitting on the couch and enjoying a baseball game on TV is a kind of watching. Or you can sit on a park bench and watch the world go by. Those are passive forms of watching.

But there's another kind of watching that is much more active. Think about a family that gathers around a young mother-to-be as she goes into labor. They watch and wait with her, as they prepare for the baby to be born. The watchers in that scenario have a real role to play. They help the mother as she struggles in labor. They pray for her. They comfort her and offer her encouragement. And they share a great expectation together as they watch and wait for the miracle of life to come forth.

We can see another type of active watching when we think about a soldier on guard duty at the edge of a city during wartime. While the city sleeps peacefully behind him, the soldier watches for any signs of danger to its inhabitants.

He watches with vigilance and protects the city's people. In olden times, a watchman would stand on the walls of the city, scanning the landscape in front of him and ready to sound the alarm if an enemy approached. His watching wasn't passive at all. It was a part of his duty to protect the city itself.

When the prophet Isaiah talks about watching in the passage above, he is referring to a very active kind of watching. The "watchmen on the walls" that Isaiah speaks about have a duty to perform. But for Isaiah, these watchmen are not watching out for danger. And the city is not any ordinary city. It is Zion, the city of God. The watchmen on the walls are watching and waiting for the return of the Lord. They know that God is preparing to do something great for His people, and they are the ones who have been appointed to proclaim the good news to the world. They have a role to play.

~

The season of the Christian year leading up to Christmas is called Advent. It's a word that means "approach" or "arrival." Advent refers to the coming of Jesus Christ, the Son of God and Messiah who arrived in the world two thousand years ago, in the form of the baby born to the Virgin Mary in Bethlehem.

When I was a kid, my brothers and sister and I all had Advent calendars. They were these big rectangular things made out of felt that hung on the wall. My Advent calendar had a Christmas tree in the middle of it, and on the top and bottom there were rows of numbered pockets. Inside the pockets were little ornaments, and each day during Advent we'd pull the ornament out for that day and pin it to the tree. As the ornaments on the tree grew day after day, we knew we were getting closer and closer to Christmas. It seems simple, but for a kid growing up in the 1980s it was an exciting way to count down the days until Christmas eve. My little sister and I would race over to our Advent calendars each morning to see who could put their ornament on the tree first.

This kind of eager expectation is exactly what Advent is about. As we remember and celebrate the birth of the Christ child each year, we spend the weeks beforehand anticipating the gift that is to come. Many churches decorate their sanctuaries with greenery and poinsettias. Some churches also put a Nativity scene outside the church building for passing cars to see. Worship services are filled with Christmas carols, and Advent wreaths are lit as a sign of the light that is coming into the world.

We observe Advent as a holy season in our churches because we're getting ready for the Christmas celebration that marks Jesus' birth. Yet Advent doesn't just point us to something that happened in the past. It also points us to the future, to the time when Jesus will return in glory. Advent has a double meaning in that it helps us both remember the incarnation of Jesus Christ in the babe of Bethlehem and anticipate his return in glory at the end of days.[1] To fully appreciate the power of Advent, we must hold both of these meanings together. We live in an "already ... not yet" time, because Christ has already come to us but not yet returned in final victory. If we only focus on the babe of Bethlehem, then we forget about the promise that "Christ has died, Christ is risen, and Christ will come again." On the other hand, if we focus only on the Second Coming, then we forget the magnificent plan of God's salvation told through the story Jesus' own life.

So when we celebrate Advent, we are watching for Jesus. We watch for the birth of the Christ child as we read familiar Scripture passages and sing beloved Christmas carols. And by watching for the birth of Jesus each year, we also watch for his expected return.

~

Have you ever wondered why Jesus came to us at all? What is it about this world that needs a Savior?

Advent takes place in the month of December, and that means that it always comes during winter. Winter is the season of the year when we watch the world grow dark and cold all around us. We see leaves fall off of trees, insects die, and animals take to the ground to escape the bitter cold of the season. Even the sun seems reluctant to offer us its light and heat, escaping over the horizon as quickly as possible in the late afternoon.

Winter reminds us that we live in a world of travail, a world where suffering and hurt are experienced by all living things. We are caught up in this predicament along with the rest of God's creation. It has been said that, of all God's creatures, humans are capable of experiencing the greatest hurt because they are the ones most capable of love. And we are capable of inflicting the greatest hurt as well. We see that when our own families are torn apart by addiction, abuse, and violence. We see it as well on a global scale in poverty, disease, and war.

One of the deepest feelings we have in our hearts is the sense that the way things are is not the way things are supposed to be. Exactly because we know what it means to love, we also know that a state of suffering is not the way God intends for the world to exist. And so we're in a dilemma. We want to find a better way for ourselves and our children, but we are trapped in a world that seems more subject to sin and evil than to grace and love.

The Apostle Paul says that it is not just we who want a better way to live, but the whole creation as well. In Romans 8:22, he speaks of the whole creation as "groaning in labor pains" as it desperately hopes to give birth to something that will change the status quo. And as the ones with the greatest ability both to love and to harm, it is we who groan the loudest.

But wait—there is good news.

~

God wants to bring something new into our human dilemma! Where we experience pain, God wants to bring healing. Where we experience hate, God wants to give us love. Where we experience tears, God wants to show us laughter. And where we experience death, God wants to give us life.

In the midst of this troubled world—where pain, brokenness, and darkness press in on every side—our cry is a cry for nothing less than salvation. This is not just salvation in the afterlife (although it certainly includes that). It is salvation now, a remedy for broken hearts and broken lives. And just as God heard the Hebrews cry out under slavery to Pharaoh, he hears the world's cry as it suffers under the burden of sin and death.

"For surely I know the plans I have for you," God tells us through the prophet Jeremiah. "Plans for your welfare and not for harm, to give you a future with hope" (Jeremiah 29:11, NRSV). The great promise of Scripture is that God is coming. As Christian believers, we look to the promise that God has given us to bring salvation from sin and death. And that promise is wrapped up in what God is doing in

9

Jesus Christ.

Christmas is about a journey and a stable, a mother and a baby, a band of shepherds and a collection of Wise Men. But it is also about us. Jesus is Emmanuel, God-with-us. And the Christmas story is a story in which we are invited to take part, because it is meant to show us the salvation that God is even now bringing about.

When I was a child, we always celebrated a "Christmas Pageant" at my grandparents' house on Christmas day. After our Christmas dinner was eaten, we would all get dressed up in costumes and act out the Nativity story. Adults would play the part of Wise Men and shepherds, and children would take the roles of Mary, Joseph, and the Innkeeper. Somebody even had a job holding the star to guide the Wise Men to the baby Jesus.

Our Christmas Pageant was always a highlight of the holiday for us. We got dressed up in fun costumes and got to act out the best story in the Bible. And in the process, the adults in our family were teaching us kids something important about Christmas itself. By repeating our little drama year after year, they were telling us that the story of Jesus' birth was not just something to be read out of the Bible, like something from a faraway time without much real bearing on the present. It is instead something in which we participate—a story where we ourselves have parts to play.

~

There is a prophet in the Old Testament named Isaiah who holds a special place in the Scriptures for Christians because of the number of his prophecies connected with the coming of Jesus. In fact, the New Testament quotes Isaiah more than any other prophet. Some of the passages in Isaiah associated with Jesus are very familiar ("Behold, a virgin shall conceive, and bear a son..." Isaiah 7:14, KJV). But others are less so. And yet, it is in some of the more unfamiliar passages that we begin to see our own roles in the Advent drama. At one point, Isaiah proclaims,

> Listen! Your watchmen lift up their voices;
>   together they shout for joy.
> When the Lord returns to Zion,
>   they will see it with their own eyes.
>   -Isaiah 52:8 (NIV)

Isaiah says that, not only is God coming to bring his people out of exile, he is also appointing watchmen to prepare for that great event. He's speaking to an Israel in exile. But perhaps he is not only talking to those of his own day and time.

When we look to the New Testament, we find, surprisingly, that we are the very watchmen God is calling for through Isaiah. The First Letter to the Thessalonians calls us "children of light" and gives us the admonition: "keep awake" (1 Thess 5:5-6). In this way, we will not "despise the words of the prophets" but be prepared for "the coming of our Lord Jesus Christ" (1 Thess 5:20-23).

And of course, Isaiah will talk about "Zion" and "Jerusalem," but we also find that Zion and Jerusalem are words that the New Testament gives to the Church. In the book of Hebrews, we find that we ourselves have "come to Mount Zion, to the heavenly Jerusalem, the city of the living God" (Hebrews 12:22, NIV). This assembly is, as Hebrews points out, none other than the Church itself.

Who are the watchmen on the walls? We are! It is God's people, then and now, who faithfully join together to prepare for the coming Savior. Just as God called Isaiah, so did God call people in Jesus' own time. And even more, God calls us now to remind the world (and even to remind God!) of the promise we have of salvation. When we come to understand that Zion and Jerusalem are images for God's people gathered in the Church, we suddenly find that it is we who are appointed to serve as watchmen for what God is doing in the world:

> On your walls, O Jerusalem,
> I have set watchmen;
> all the day and all the night
> they shall never be silent.
> You who put the Lord in
> remembrance,
> take no rest
> and give him no rest
> until he establishes Jerusalem
> and makes it a praise in the earth.
> -Isaiah 62:6-7

So much of what we see in the Old Testament prophets is focused on what *God* is going to do. But here we see Isaiah prophesy about what God's *people* will do for and with God.[2]

~

It is an exciting thing to think that, long before Bethlehem, God was working to prepare the world for its Savior. And it is doubly exciting to know that God has called us into that great drama. For indeed, the world needs watchmen now more than ever. It needs a Church full of people who accept their calling to be witnesses to the lost and hurting of this world. It needs those who will join together on the walls, scanning the horizon and preparing to proclaim the coming of the Lord. It needs a people full of hope for what God has promised to do.

So as we turn to the great Advent story for the next few weeks, we will look more deeply at how God uses watchmen on the walls, serving as a reminder of what is coming soon. Foretold in prophecies centuries before his birth, at a time when God's covenant people were suffering in exile, the advent (or coming) of Jesus into the world is God's answer to all the pain and heartache the world has known. It is an answer that will eventually say a decisive 'no' to death and a 'yes' to life.

Those who watch are those who wait. God's watchmen are waiters, but they aren't waiting for just anything. They are waiting for the best thing, the thing that God is getting ready to do.

In our culture it is often not easy to wait. We live in a fast-food, have-it-your-way society. We want instant gratification. We want what we want now, and we don't want to have to stand in line for it! Needless to say, that is not an attitude that makes for much patience. So it is all the more important that we understand that our waiting is an active waiting. When we pray for the coming of the Christ child, we pray with hope and with expectation.

The spiritual writer Henri Nouwen believed that the story of Jesus' birth was all about how to wait eagerly but with patience. When he was reflecting on Jesus' birth story in the Gospel of Luke, he wrote, "Waiting, as we see it in [Luke] is waiting with a sense of promise." That kind of waiting, to Nouwen, was a waiting in the midst of God's promise. "We can only really wait if what we are waiting for has already begun for us," Nouwen says. "So waiting is never a movement from nothing to something. It is always a movement from something to something more."[3] As Nouwen saw it, that kind of waiting is anything but passive. It is full of activity and hope, and it is always directed to the promise that God has given.

Psalm 130 puts it this way:

> I wait for the LORD, my soul waits,
>   and in his word I hope;
> my soul waits for the Lord
>   more than watchmen for the morning,
>   more than watchmen for the morning.
> O Israel, hope in the LORD!
>   For with the LORD there is steadfast love,
>   and with him is plentiful redemption.
> And he will redeem Israel
>   from all his iniquities.

Our restless waiting in the world is often filled with anxiety because we think we are somehow going to be left unfulfilled if we can't have what we want, when we want it. But the story of Advent is that One is coming who will give us all we could ever need and more. So waiting in an Advent context is exciting because we know we can count on what is promised. We can watch with joy and wait with hope.

Are you watching?

DISCUSSION GUIDE

Prayer:

O God of hope, give us eyes to see and ears to hear what you have to show us as we prepare for the coming of our Savior. Prepare us to be your watchmen on the walls, and give us a role to play in your great kingdom-building story. Grant us the blessing of your Holy Spirit, that we may embark upon this study with expectation and joy, ready to proclaim the salvation of Jesus to all people. Amen.

Questions for discussion:

1. During the season of Advent, how are we called to be open to the ways that Jesus' love is being born all around us?

2. What would it mean for you to be a watchman on the walls for God during this Advent? What are you watching for this time of year?

3. Do you have any traditions in your family that help you to understand the Advent season better?

4. Do you find it hard to wait patiently for the things in your life that you really want? How can your faith help you to wait more patiently in your life?

5. Are you watching?

NOTES

[1] The New Westminster Dictionary makes this point well: "Advent has come to mark preparation for the coming of Christ in a double manner, first in his incarnation as the babe of Bethlehem, which is obvious, and in his second coming at the end of time..." See J.G. Davies, ed., *The New Westminster Dictionary of Liturgy and Worship* (Philadelphia: The Westminster Press, 1986), 2.

[2] One commentator explains that the watchmen in this passage are "dispatched by the prophet to ceaselessly keep God on notice about Zion's establishment in the sight of the nations." See Christopher R. Seitz, *Isaiah 40-66*, in Volume VI of *The New Interpreter's Bible* (Nashville: Abingdon Press, 2001), 515.

[3] Henri J.M. Nouwen, "A Spirituality of Waiting: Being Alert to God's Presence in Our Lives," in *Weavings: A Journal of the Christian Spiritual Life* 2:1 (January/February 1987), 9.

Chapter Two
Mary's Encounter

Luke 1:26-38

I was taking my 8-year old daughter Alice to basketball practice one night not long ago. It was dark and raining, and on the way to the church gym we realized that we had forgotten to bring her water bottle. So instead of parking and walking in together, I pulled up to the curb at the gym entrance.

"Go ahead and hop out," I said. "You can go on in to practice, and I'll run down the street and pick up a bottle of water for you."

"Um ... okay," she said. Then she paused with her hand on the door handle.

I noticed her hesitation. "What is it?" I said.

She looked back at me and then out at the rainy night. "That just makes me a little bit scared," she said.

To me, it seemed like such a small thing: hop out of the truck, walk the 20 feet to the gym entrance while I watched, and open the door to join her teammates. I would be back with her water in just a few minutes. But to Alice, it was a scenario that made her feel nervous, frightened, alone. The night was dark, the rain was cold, and there would be no dad beside her to hold her hand.

Alice did jump out of the truck after a couple of encouraging words, and I watched her small form move from the dark of the rainy night into the warm light of the gymnasium. Everything was going to be ok. As I watched her go, my thoughts turned to another young girl in a scary situation: the Virgin Mary, who was visited suddenly by an angel named Gabriel and given startling news. Mary was a few years older than Alice was that night at the gym, but only a few. She was still very young, and very vulnerable. What would Mary have felt like on that strange night? What kind of emotions must have been coursing through her as she heard the angel's message, and realized the risky position she was about to be put in?

~

Our watching begins in a little village called Nazareth, about 15 miles from the freshwater lake known as the Sea of Galilee. It begins with a young Jewish girl named Mary, who was engaged to be married to a local man, a woodworker named Joseph. She was probably no more than 14 or 15 years old. And one day, she had a most unusual encounter. An encounter with an angel.

It's not always clear what angels look like when they show up in the Bible. When the three mysterious visitors came to meet Abraham and Sarah at the Oaks of Mamre, they appeared as ordinary men[1]. Yet the angels in the vision of the prophet Isaiah during his call story had six wings each and a fiery appearance[2]. (The word "seraphim" is taken from the Hebrew word for flames.) It does seem like, more often than not, the experience of meeting an angel can be frightening. Mary's encounter starts out in a way that would make you think that anyway. "Do not be afraid, Mary," the angel said. "You have found favor with God."

His name was Gabriel. He's one of two good angels actually named in the Bible—along with Michael.[3] (Because of that the two are usually called archangels.) Like all angels, Gabriel's primary role is to serve as a messenger for God. And the message he had to deliver to Mary was going to

18

turn her world upside down. In fact, it was going to turn the whole world upside down.

"You will conceive and give birth to a son, and you are to call him Jesus," Gabriel told her. "He will be great and will be called Son of the Most High." He went on: "The Lord God will give him the throne of his father, David, and he will reign over Jacob's descendants forever. His kingdom will never end."

Both the angel's appearance and message put Mary on an emotional roller coaster. Now sometimes our tendency is to read the story of Gabriel's visit to Mary in such a way that we think of Mary as just passively accepting everything that Gabriel says. A passive attitude doesn't really fit with what we know about Mary as a person, though. This is the woman who would later rush back to Jerusalem in a huff when she realized her twelve-year old son had stayed behind after the Passover was ended. *"Son, why have you treated us like this?"* she scolded him once she finally found him. It's also the same Mary who would not flinch from standing at the foot of the cross some twenty years later when that same son was being crucified. In other words, she was strong and resilient and wasn't prone to be passive about anything. Sure, I can imagine the first thing Mary felt when Gabriel showed up in her bedroom was fear. (Who wouldn't be frightened by an angel appearing out of nowhere??) But pretty soon her fear moved to curiosity. "How will this be," she said to Gabriel, "since I am a virgin?"

He answered her: "The Holy Spirit will come upon you, and the power of the Most High will overshadow you. So the holy one to be born will be called the Son of God." Then, Mary answers, and her reply demonstrates her confidence in who she is and who God is. "I am the Lord's servant," she says. "May it be to me as you have said." Her answer to Gabriel is full of strength. It is full of resilience. It is a powerful statement of faith. She didn't answer him by trying to avoid God's plan for her life. There was no, "I don't want this!" or "I can't handle this responsibility." She heard the angel's message, and with a heart of courage she proclaimed her acceptance and embrace of who God called her to be: "*I am the Lord's servant.*" It's a faith statement. When she follows with, "Let it be to me as you have said," she is essentially stepping forward from that faith into God's future for her. She is ready to be a vessel for God's work and God's power.

~

Of course, Mary's willing acceptance of the angel's message does not mean that her life wasn't about to get a lot more complicated. In fact it is not an exaggeration to say that Gabriel's message put her in real danger. Mary was a vulnerable, unwed teenage girl. One minute she had great hopes of a marriage to a local carpenter, assuring her of economic stability and the hope of children someday of her own. The next minute she knew she was about to become pregnant, and she had nothing but an unbelievable story about a visit by an angel to defend herself with. She lived in a society where unwed mothers were looked down upon, particularly those who became pregnant by someone other than the man to whom they were pledged to marry. The law found in Deuteronomy 22:23-24 states, "If a man happens to meet in a town a virgin pledged to be married and he sleeps with her, you shall take both of them to the gate of that town and stone them to death—the girl because she was in a town and did not scream for help, and the man because he violated another man's wife. You must purge the evil from among you." Mary would not have been guilty of that, of course, but how could she have proved it? Her pregnancy would become known in time, and Joseph would be sure that he was not the father. There was no social safety net on which she could rely, and the assumptions everyone was sure to make would cause her to be an outcast in her own town.

It's in that context that the quality of Mary's faith becomes clear. I've never known whether God chose Mary because he knew the kind of character she had on the front end, or whether her character was forged through the experience of receiving God's favor and having to respond with complete trust and commitment. Regardless of which it is, what is clear is that Mary was the perfect vessel to conceive and give birth to the Savior of the world. Her son would be none other than God incarnate, the divine being in human flesh. And so from the time of the early church, Mary has carried the most noble of titles—"theotokos," the bearer of God.

There's a word often used to describe the story of Jesus' coming into the world: scandal. It's scandalous to think that the Creator of the world and Lord of all would come into the creation in the form of a helpless baby. It's a scandal that the king who would sit on David's throne would be born not in a palace but rather in a stable. It's all a huge scandal—Jesus' life, his ministry, his death, and his resurrection. He comes to bless the poor, heal the sick, and raise the dead. He is hailed as the Son of David when he enters Jerusalem, but his throne turns out to be a cross. And the ultimate victory he wins comes through his own death. In all of that, the scandal begins with his mother Mary. She is placed in an impossible predicament and put in real personal danger ... why? Perhaps it is exactly to reveal that God uses the humble, the poor, and the weak to bring about his kingdom on earth. In the story of Jesus, that truth is revealed first of all in the person of Mary herself, and in the circumstances by which she brought the Savior of mankind into this world.

~

The encounter between Gabriel and Mary has traditionally been called the "annunciation," because it is the place where Gabriel *announces* to Mary that she is going to give birth to the Christ child. In much of Christian art thorough the centuries, painters have depicted their meeting in an almost formulaic way. The winged angel is floating above Mary, often gesturing with one hand as he delivers his message. (Sometimes Gabriel kneels before Mary, but he is always recognizable as an angel with his large feathered wings, long hair, and robes.) Mary is usually sitting or kneeling, and she often looks down at the ground in an attitude of submission. Both Mary and Gabriel typically have halos around their heads to denote their holiness.

Public Domain Image

There is one depiction of the annunciation, however, that is striking in the way it defies the usual conventions. It is a version that was painted by the American artist Henry Ossawa Tanner in 1898.

Tanner's painting of the *The Annunciation* does not feature a Gabriel who would be recognizable by any standard notion of what an angel should look like. He is instead a bright, golden shaft of light that illuminates the entire scene. By using such a strange but striking image, Tanner reminds us of how people in the Bible often react to the visit of an angel: with outright fear. When an angel appeared to Zechariah to tell him that his wife Elizabeth would give birth to John the Baptist, he was "gripped with fear" (Luke 1:12). And when the angel arrived in the field to tell the shepherds about the good news of Jesus' birth, they were "terrified" (Luke 2:9). Mary herself was frightened enough when Gabriel appeared in her room that he had to calm her by saying, "Do not be afraid, Mary. You have found favor with God" (Luke 1:30). We don't in fact know what form the angel took—only that he spoke in language understandable to his audience. Whatever his appearance was like, though, it was frightening to the people he was sent to visit.

The Mary that we see in Henry Ossawa Tanner's depiction of *The Annunciation* is past her initial fear, and it is the detail Tanner has given her that makes the painting so powerful. This is not the stylized or romanticized Virgin of so many *Annunciations* from previous centuries. Tanner's Mary is a Jewish peasant girl, sitting on a simple bed and clothed in an old gray linen garment. Her brown hair is tied back and her hands are clasped in front of her. Her shoulders are slightly hunched and her face slightly apprehensive as she looks at the angel. The toes of her left foot peak out from under her garment, emphasizing the almost childlike nature of the girl who even at that moment was hearing the message that she was to bear the Son of God.

David Neff of *Christianity Today* points out that one of the signal features of Henry Ossawa Tanner's religious paintings is his tendency to want to draw the viewer into the scene. Tanner was the son of a bishop in the African Methodist Episcopal Church, and he had a strong faith in God. His illustration of biblical scenes was meant to bring us into contact with the God who stood at their center. "Tanner wanted to put us, the viewers, in the frame," Neff says, "for those stories are addressed to us and are about us." You see this again and again in Tanner's paintings, and you certainly see it in *The Annunciation*. We look into the room practically standing on the angel's side, so that Mary is facing us even as her gaze is directed to the brilliant light of the angel's form. Neff says, "Because Mary is turned toward us, we share her reaction, listening with her for the divine Word as she receives the angel's message and the Spirit's overshadowing."[4] It is a reminder to us once again that Mary's story is our story. We are meant to embrace her encounter with the angel Gabriel because the salvation he was announcing to her is a salvation meant for us. We are the watchmen on the walls.

~

As the Gospel of Luke tells the story, the encounter between Gabriel and Mary moves progressively from the cosmic to the concrete.[5] Luke 1:26-27 says, "In the sixth month, the angel Gabriel was sent by God to a town in Galilee called Nazareth, to a virgin engaged to a man whose name was Joseph, of the house of David. The virgin's name was Mary." Gabriel stands in the presence of God, and then God calls Gabriel to stand in the presence of Mary. The rhythm of his movement from the cosmic to the concrete looks like this:

Sent from God →
    to a town in Galilee →
        called Nazareth →
            to a virgin named Mary.

This is the beginning of our story with Jesus. We go with Gabriel, to watch over his shoulder as he carries out his mission. We are there, in the earthy setting of a humble Galilean home, in the presence of an angel and a young girl, talking by lamplight in the quiet of evening. We hear him deliver the monumental news that this young girl will give birth to a Savior. Then we hear her response, quiet but resolute, as she accepts with pure faith the message that her life will never be the same again. We take our place upon the walls and stand as watchmen for the coming of the Lord. "I have posted watchmen on your walls, Jerusalem!" the prophet Isaiah says. "They will never be silent day or night."

We are those called to watch for the birth of our Messiah, ready to cry out with joy when the light of his glory comes into the world.

DISCUSSION GUIDE

Prayer:

Father in heaven, you called your servant Mary to be the mother of our Savior. Help us to share in her strong faith. Give us the same willingness to be called according to your purpose. By the power of your Holy Spirit, let us always be awake and aware to the work you are doing in our world. In Jesus' name, Amen.

Questions for discussion:

1. What do you think it was like for Mary when Gabriel appeared to her all of a sudden? If you put yourself in her place, what would you have been feeling?

2. How would you describe the faith that Mary demonstrates in her encounter with the angel? What would it look like for you to have faith like that?

3. What does it say about God that he chose to come into the world as the child of a young peasant teenage girl? What does that mean for how we are called to follow him?

4. Have you ever encountered an angel? What was it like?

5. Are you watching?

NOTES

1 Genesis 18:1-15.

2 Isaiah 6:1-7

3 The only two good angels ever mentioned by name in the Bible are Gabriel and Michael. Gabriel is found in Daniel 8:15-26 and 9:21-27; and Luke 1:11-20, 26-38, while Michael is found in Daniel 10:13, 21 and 12:1; Jude 9; and Revelation 12:7. Evil angels are also mentioned, with Satan being the best known. See Paul Achtemeier, ed., *HarperCollins Bible Dictionary* (New York: HarperCollins, 1996), 33-34, 356, and 682. Other angels are mentioned in the Apocrypha.

4 David Neff, "Preacher with a Paintbrush," *Christianity Today* (June 3, 2015).Online at:
https://www.christianitytoday.com/ct/2015/may/preacher-with-paintbrush.html (accessed February 12, 2019).

5 This movement "from general to specific" is noted by R. Alan Culpepper, *The Gospel of Luke*, in Volume IX of *The New Interpreter's Bible* (Nashville: Abingdon Press, 1995), 51.

Chapter Three
Joseph's Challenge

Matthew 1:1-25; 2:13-23

On May 6, 1954, Roger Bannister did something that no one in history had ever done before. He ran a mile in 3 minutes 59.4 seconds, breaking the 4-minute mile barrier.[1] There's a famous photo of Bannister by Norman Potter taken at the moment he crosses the finish line at Oxford's Iffley Road track. His head is back and his mouth open, and he's throwing himself through the tape with every ounce of energy he has left. When you see that picture, you get the sense that Bannister is accomplishing something monumental and heroic. He looks like a solitary champion crashing through a barrier previously thought impossible to break.

Chronicle / Alamy Stock Photo. Used by permission.

The only problem with that image of Bannister as the solitary hero is that he didn't accomplish the great feat of the 4-minute mile by himself at all. The Norman Potter photo is deceiving. When Bannister began the race that would turn him into a household name, he had two pace men running with him—one in front and one behind. Their names were Chris Brasher and Chris Chataway, and they were both excellent runners in their own right.

Brasher and Chataway don't show up in the famous finish line photo because, by that point, they had already done their jobs. They were the ones responsible for setting just the right pace so that Bannister would have a chance to break the record in the last few hundred yards before the finish line. Chris Brasher took the lead in the race for the first half-mile, and while he was running Bannister urged him to go faster.[2] But Brasher held his pace, knowing that he had to go just fast enough (but not too fast) if Bannister was going to have to have a chance to break the record at the end. On the third time around the track, Chris Chataway took over and led for a lap while Brasher fell back. Then, finally, Bannister shot forward with a powerful kick in the final lap and broke the record. Just like it was planned to happen.

The role of a pace man is not glamorous, but it is important. It isn't the kind of job that is going to get you remembered for all time. It is rather the quintessential supporting role: the guy who is there to help somebody else accomplish something great and noteworthy. That was the role Chris Brasher and Chris Chataway were called to play. And if it weren't for them, Roger Bannister never would have broken the record at all.

When we look at the figure of Joseph in the Advent

story, we see a character who shares some similarities with Chris Brasher and Chris Chataway. He was part of a great story, just as they were. But just like them, his role was a supporting one. We usually think of the stars of the story as being the Virgin Mary and the baby Jesus. Joseph was there, though, doing his part to make sure that the race was going to be won. He set the pace to make sure that the holy family would make it to Bethlehem before time had come for Jesus to be born. He later led his wife and child down into Egypt to escape the wrath of King Herod. And he brought them up again into Israel to settle in Nazareth after the threat of Herod had passed from the scene, so that Jesus could grow up and become a man. Without Joseph, Jesus would never have been able to do all that God had called him to do.

As we stand watching on the walls during the Advent story, Joseph's experience should raise questions in our minds about what things must have been like for him. What must it have been like for his marriage (and indeed, his whole life) to have been so radically changed at a moment's notice? How did it make him feel to be called upon to be the stepfather and protector to the Savior of the whole world? How did he meet a challenge he never sought out, to fulfill a mission he never imagined he'd be called to pursue?

~

One of the unique things about the Advent story is the way it is divided up between two different gospels: Luke and Matthew. Luke's focus is on the experience of Mary. He includes her family connection to Elizabeth and Zechariah. It's Luke that tells us about the Roman census and the difficult journey from Nazareth to Bethlehem prior to Jesus' birth. Luke also introduces us to the shepherds on the night that Jesus is born.

Matthew tells the story with some different accents. He shines the spotlight on Joseph and his role in the birth of Jesus. Whereas Luke includes the shepherds, Matthew tells us about the visit of the Wise Men. Matthew also tells of a journey just like Luke, but the journey that he tells about is the flight to Egypt to escape the evil King Herod in the months following Jesus' birth.

In all the ways that it focuses on Joseph, Matthew's gospel is drawing out Joseph's challenging role as the fatherly guardian and protector of both Mary and Jesus. When Mary was discovered to be pregnant prior to their marriage, it must have caused enormous pain and anguish for Joseph. He would come to understand the miraculous circumstances of that pregnancy later on, but Joseph was only human and his first reaction must surely have been to recoil with a sense of betrayal. Yet he had no desire to publicly shame or humiliate Mary—he simply "resolved to divorce her quietly," as it says in Matthew 1:19. Then, just as Mary herself had an angelic encounter, Joseph is visited by an angel as well. In a dream one night, the angel tells Joseph, "Joseph, son of David, do not fear to take Mary as your wife, for that which is conceived in her is from the Holy Spirit. She will bear a son, and you shall call his name Jesus, for he will save his people from their sins." (Matthew 1:20b-21). With those words, we can see Joseph's challenge take form: he first has to trust God enough to walk forward into a marriage that is going to look very different than the one he had planned or wanted; then he has to figure out how to raise and protect the child who will be no less than the Messiah and Savior of the world.

It is a huge challenge, but it is one that Joseph resolves

to meet: "When Joseph woke from sleep," the Bible says, "he did as the angel of the Lord commanded him and took Mary home as his wife" (Matthew 1:24, NIV). Mary often receives deserving praise for the faithfulness she shows in accepting God's plan for her. We tend to give Joseph less attention, but his reaction to the message delivered by the angel is no less praiseworthy. He moves from alienation to embrace with respect to Mary. He gets brought into God's master plan for salvation through Jesus, and he accepts the place God has for him in it.

~

Joseph's role as the supporting cast of the Advent story means that he is a little bit of an enigma. He always has been. He is necessary, yet in many ways not well known. He's strong yet largely silent. Whereas Mary both speaks and sings in the Nativity story, Joseph never utters a word. He is spoken about, but he never actually speaks.

That mysterious aspect to his personality goes beyond the Advent story too. As the gospels move forward in telling about Jesus' life, Joseph just sort of ... fades away. The last time he plays an active role in the story of Jesus' life is during the family's trip to Jerusalem for the Passover when Jesus was 12 years old. After that, the only place Joseph is even mentioned in passing is when people are questioning Jesus and say, "Isn't this the carpenter's son?" (Matthew 13:55).[3] That isn't the case with Mary, of course. She is present throughout Jesus' ministry and even follows him to Jerusalem towards the end of his life. As Jesus was dying on the cross, his mother was there with the disciple John at the scene (John 19:25-27). After Jesus' resurrection and ascension into heaven, Mary stayed with the disciples in Jerusalem and became part of the early church (Acts 1:14).

And we know from later church history that Mary survived for many years and likely settled in the city of Ephesus on the western coast of Asia Minor.[4] With Joseph, though, no such details exist. He played his part and then he passed from the scene.

Yet while Joseph's personality remains obscure, what he represents is crucial to Jesus' identity as the Messiah. Back when King David sat on the throne about a thousand years before Jesus, God had blessed him and his royal house with an eternal blessing. The Lord promised to establish a house for David, with his descendants to reign in succession after him. "Your house and your kingdom will endure forever before me," God said to David through the prophet Nathan. "Your throne will be established forever" (2 Samuel 7:16, NIV).

That promise meant that the Messiah would be a Davidic Messiah. He would come from the line of David's descendants. And he would come to restore David's throne and bring justice to God's own people. So while the people of Israel didn't know when or how their Messiah would come, they did know that when he came he would be inextricably connected to King David. He would, in fact, be the new David who came to make good on the promises of the past and lead Israel into a hopeful future.

Knowing that, the statement in the Gospel of Luke that Joseph was "of the house and lineage of David" (Luke 2:4) takes on a special significance. Joseph was not Jesus' biological father. But the fact that God had chosen Joseph to be his adoptive father and his guardian meant that Jesus was to be a part of Joseph's house—and that house was the House of David. The Gospel of Matthew's focus on Joseph begins in the very first verse of the very first

35

chapter—which tells us, "The book of the genealogy of Jesus Christ, the son of David" (Matthew 1:1). A genealogy follows from that first line, which traces the ancestry of Jesus from Abraham, through David, and down to Joseph. Matthew does that because he wants to show who Jesus is: the son of Joseph, and through him, the son of King David himself. He has the connection to Israel's greatest king that the Messiah has to have in order to be the Messiah at all.

Does Jesus' connection to David through Joseph really matter, or is it just a little piece of Bible trivia? It does matter, and it matters very much. The fact that Jesus comes from David's line shows us that God remains true to his promises. Turn to psalm 136 and you'll find that it has 26 verses in it, and 26 times it repeats the phrase, "for his steadfast love endures forever." That is an affirmation that God's love is ever-present and enduring. His promises are sure and true. He will never abandon or forsake his people.

So Joseph's presence in the Advent story is a reminder to us of the way God loves us. Sometimes it can seem hard to understand how God is at work in our lives. Sometimes we wish things were just more plainly in view. But if God can make good on a thousand-year old promise to King David by sending his Son, Jesus, into the world, then we can be assured that he will make good on his promises to us. Like Joseph, we are called to trust that God's provision for us will be sufficient and that the story God will write for our lives is better than anything we could ever craft on our own.

~

As we watch from the walls as the character of Joseph plays his part in the Christmas drama, how does his witness draw us into the story? Personally, I find myself connecting especially with Joseph's "everyman" status. There just

36

doesn't seem to be anything particularly special about him other than his trust and obedience to God's calling in the midst of his already-made plans and his willingness to rise to the challenge of what that calling represents. Joseph has been called the "forgotten man of Christmas."[5] He's the one who gets lost amidst the mother-and-child intimacy of Mary and Jesus, and amidst the drama of the angels and shining stars in the night sky.

Yet it is in that very everyman quality that we also find an important truth that pertains not only to Joseph but to every ordinary believer that God has called from his time to our own. When the angel met Joseph in his dream, it was God's way of saying to him, "I need you to be my watchman on the walls. I need you to watch over Mary whom I have chosen, and Jesus my Son. I need you to be the guardian of the Savior." In sending the angel to plain old Joseph, the carpenter from a little village in the Galilee, God was showing that he could use anyone, in any circumstance, to accomplish his purposes in the world.

God can use us, too. He does, in fact. All the time. We may doubt that God would ever choose someone as plain and ordinary as *us*, but God doesn't doubt that at all. In 1 Corinthians 1:26-29 (NIV), the Apostle Paul writes,

> Brothers and sisters, think of what you were when you were called. Not many of you were wise by human standards; not many were influential; not many were of noble birth. But God chose the foolish things of the world to shame the wise; God chose the weak things of the world to shame the strong. He chose the lowly things of this world and the despised things—and the things that are

not—to nullify the things that are, so that no one may boast before him.

What an encouragement! Have you ever thought you weren't smart enough, strong enough, or powerful enough? Well guess what—none of that is a barrier to God's plan for the world **or** God's plan for your life. Put your trust in him and obey him (as Joseph did) and there is no telling what God will do with you.

There is one little caveat that Joseph's witness gives us, and it's an important one. We don't actually get to choose the way that God is going to call us. Sometimes that call will involve a real challenge to our settled notions about what our lives should look like. That was certainly the case for Joseph, and it may well be the case for us. But if Joseph's story tells us anything, it is that God's plans are infinitely better than anything we could ever imagine. So much better, in fact, that they'll cause us to offer up our entire lives just to be a part of them.

DISCUSSION GUIDE

Prayer:

Holy and gracious God, you sometimes show up in the most unexpected ways. Give us hearts that are ready to receive you however you come into our lives. Grant us also the humility to accept the role that you want us to fill in the building of your kingdom. By your Spirit, give us the courage to face whatever comes our way and the trust to know that you are with us. Amen.

Questions for discussion:

1. What do you think Joseph's most important duty is? As the "supporting cast" of the Advent story, how is Joseph a crucial part of what God is doing?

2. We don't always get to choose how God is going to call us. Have you ever had the sense that you were called to do something that you never expected or asked for? What was that like?

3. Have you ever felt like your life was caught up in a larger story, with a purpose that went beyond just you? Was that a strange experience to have? How did it affect your relationship with Jesus?

4. Are you watching?

NOTES

[1] Ian Chadband, "The story of runner Roger Bannister, the 'Greatest Living Englishman,'" ESPN.com (March 7, 2018); online at: http://www.espn.com/sports/endurance/story/_/id/22677426/the-story-runner-roger-bannister-greatest-living-englishman (accessed May 31, 2019).

[2] David Walsh, "Golden Pioneer: Chris Brasher's creation of the London Marathon is a testament to the vision and competitive urge that drove him on," *The Sunday Times* (March 2, 2003); online at: https://www.thetimes.co.uk/article/golden-pioneer-2x9q3jnbld6 (accessed November 7, 2019).

[3] In the Gospel of John, the question is posed a little differently: "Is not this Jesus, the son of Joseph, whose father and mother we know?" (John 6:42).

[4] Church tradition has held from an early time that Mary eventually emigrated to Ephesus with John the Apostle. The most direct historical evidence for this comes from the words of John 20:27, which state that John ("the disciple whom Jesus loved") took Mary into his home following the crucifixion. We know (e.g., from Eusebius' *Church History* 3.1 and 3.18-20) that John went to Ephesus and lived there for many years.

[5] Joel C. Gregory, "The Forgotten Man of Christmas," *Preaching Today* (December 2014); available online at: https://www.preachingtoday.com/sermons/sermons/2014/december/forgotten-man-christmas.html (accessed October 10, 2019).

Chapter Four
Elizabeth's Surprise

Luke 1:5-25, 39-80

The Bible is full of stories of women who have trouble getting pregnant. We find that theme occurring in the lives of each of the three patriarchs and their wives: Abraham and Sarah had lived together for decades with no children before God gave them Isaac. He was born when Sarah was more than 90 years old. Later on, Isaac married Rebekah, but she too was barren until God caused her to conceive in response to Isaac's prayer. One of their sons, Jacob, married the sisters Leah and Rachel. Rachel had trouble conceiving, which led indirectly to a great deal of family discord, though God did eventually grant her children as well.

In the years following the Israelites' escape from Egypt and the entrance into the Promised Land, the theme of barrenness continues. In the time of the Judges, Manoah and his wife were not able to have children until an angel of the Lord appeared to her and promised her a son, the hero Samson. Then later on, Elkanah and Hannah experienced trouble conceiving, and Hannah repeatedly poured out her heart before God in prayers and tears. She promised the Lord that she would dedicate her son to God's service if only her prayer was answered and she became pregnant. God heard her prayer, and she gave birth to Samuel, who became one of the greatest prophets that ever lived.

The Gospel of Luke begins by introducing us to the figures of Elizabeth and Zechariah—a couple devoted to one another who stood in the long line of biblical figures that wanted a child but were unable to have one. They were outstanding people. Luke says that they "were both righteous before God, walking blamelessly in all the commandments and statutes of the Lord" (Luke 1:6). Yet they had been childless throughout their marriage, and they had little prospect of having any children because they were "advanced in years."

Yet just as Old Testament figures like Sarah and Hannah would find themselves the recipients of God's miraculous work, so too would Elizabeth. The angel Gabriel appeared one day to her husband Zechariah as he was ministering in the Temple—he was a priest. Gabriel told him that their prayers had been heard by God and that Elizabeth was going to become pregnant. He told Zechariah that they were to name their child John, and that he would become a great prophet: "He will turn many of the children of Israel to the Lord their God," Gabriel said. "And God will go before him in the spirit and power of Elijah, to turn the hearts of the fathers to their children, and the disobedient to the wisdom of the just, to make ready for the Lord a people prepared" (Luke 1:16-17).

What news! It was surely the biggest surprise of Elizabeth and Zechariah's life. The inability to conceive children carried a deep social stigma in Jewish society at the time. Though Zechariah and Elizabeth were known as upstanding and respectable people otherwise, Elizabeth's barrenness would have been considered as "a tragedy, a disgrace, and even a sign of God's punishment."[1] Yet now, long after the age when Elizabeth would have expected to be able to have a baby, an angel appears and tells them that the deepest prayer of their hearts is going to be answered. It was so shocking, in fact, that Zechariah had a hard time believing the message from God even though Gabriel was standing right there in front of him delivering it. For her part, Elizabeth withdrew and kept herself hidden in private for five months after she conceived. It must have been difficult to come to grips with what was happening to them. Yet the baby in Elizabeth's womb—who would become known later on as John the Baptist—was a sign that God's favor was resting upon them.

~

Mary had her own angelic visitation, of course. And as soon as Gabriel left her, Mary realized that what she most needed to do was to get out of town. Gabriel had delivered such earth-shattering news to Mary that it threatened to overwhelm her. She needed someone she could turn to—a trusted mentor who would be able to speak to her out of wisdom and experience. Her whole world was coming crashing down around her, and she needed a safe harbor where she could take some time and sort things out.

The person she chose was Elizabeth, her cousin. Luke tells us, "In those days Mary arose and went with haste into the hill country, to a town in Judah, and she entered the house of Zechariah and greeted Elizabeth" (1:39-40). When Mary walked into their home, Elizabeth got her second major surprise. The angel had told Zechariah that their son John would be "filled with the Holy Spirit, even from his mother's womb" (Luke 1:15). Elizabeth found out how true that promise was when she heard Mary's voice, because right at that moment her baby leaped in her womb. Elizabeth cried out immediately and she, too, was filled with the Holy Spirit.

"Jump for Joy" by Corby Eisbacher. www.artbycorby.etsy.com. Used by permission.

There is a wonderful watercolor painting that captures the moment that Mary greeted Elizabeth called *Jump for Joy* that was painted by contemporary artist Corby Eisbacher. It shows Elizabeth with her hand on Mary's stomach, and her head is thrown back in laughter. Both women have huge smiles on their faces, as if they are reveling in the work that God is doing through them. The image evokes Elizabeth's words to Mary at that moment: "Blessed are you among women, and blessed is the fruit of your womb! And why is this granted to me that the mother of my Lord should come to me? For behold, when the sound of your greeting came to my ears, the baby in my womb leaped for joy" (Luke 1:42-44).

I believe that the moment they came together was hugely significant for them, yet in different ways. For Mary, there had to have been a great sense of relief at being able to relax and rest in the home of a woman she loved and trusted. For Elizabeth, she suddenly had an answer to why God would grant her a son in her old age and what his mission would be—he would be the herald for the Messiah himself. Elizabeth also knew from that point on that she was connected to Mary by more than just blood kinship. To her delight and surprise, she realized that they were also connected by being chosen to play important roles in God's purposes for the world.

~

When I was in the fifth grade, my Sunday school teacher was a young man named Chip Dortch. He was just 25 years old when he agreed to be our teacher. For a class of fifth grade boys and girls, it was amazing! We assumed that we would get somebody's grandmother or grandfather as a teacher, and here we had gotten a guy who almost young enough to be our older brother. We loved it.

That was a wonderful year for a bunch of kids in Sunday school. But the best was still yet to come. Because at the end of the year, we begged and pleaded with Chip to move up with us and be our sixth grade teacher also. And he agreed! So we got to stick with Chip for a second year too, until it was time for us to graduate up to junior high youth group. His level of commitment was amazing, and he showed us week in and week out that he cared about us.

Now here's the thing: I don't remember much of anything about the lessons or the biblical characters that we focused on during those fifth and sixth grade years. It was over 30 years ago for me. I don't remember what we did on any single individual week. But you know what I do remember? I remember how much Chip cared about us. And how he was a mentor to us. I remember that this young guy who could have been doing anything with his time decided to give it to us. And I remember how elated we all were when he told us he was going to level up with us and stick with us for a second year. He was committed to us, and it made a difference to every single kid in the class.

Sometimes when we think about how we are growing as disciples, we can tend to focus on the content of what we are doing. We want to learn more about the Bible. We want to learn how to pray better. It's true that those things are important. But there's something equally as important if not more so: it's our relationships with other believers. Discipleship is about relationships as much as anything. When Jesus gave us the two great Commandments, they were not commandments that we have a "head knowledge" of God and our neighbor. His commandments to us were that we love God and love our neighbor. The language of our faith is the language of relationships.

The gift that Elizabeth gave her young cousin Mary was the gift of relationship. Elizabeth was older than Mary, and she was further along in her pregnancy. The Bible doesn't say exactly why Mary went to see her, but it does say that Mary went "with haste" to Elizabeth's home shortly after the angel Gabriel visited her. We can imagine that part of Mary's motivation was anxiety and a deep sense of uncertainty: as a teenage girl who had become pregnant by means other than her husband, her reputation and possibly her very life were in danger. She didn't know at the time whether Joseph would stay with her or abandon her. She needed to be with someone that she trusted who could offer her wisdom and care.

Elizabeth had a number of surprises that came her way. The first was the news that she was going to become pregnant after years of suffering from barrenness. The second was the major kick she got from her Spirit-filled son

John inside her womb. But the greatest surprise of all was that, in her young cousin Mary, she suddenly came face-to-face with the mother of her own Savior. Luke signals that fact by telling us that it was at that moment that Elizabeth was filled with the Holy Spirit. It's then that she pronounces her blessing over Mary.

For Mary, those words must have cascaded down upon her with a profound sense of relief. Mary was likely very nervous and afraid about what sort of reception she would get when she arrived at Elizabeth's house. (Would she believe Mary's story about her visit from the angel? Or, would she react with horror and throw Mary out of her house?) To hear Elizabeth embrace her with joy and call her blessed must have been sweeter than anything Mary could have hoped for.

It is surely true that the Holy Spirit moved Elizabeth to speak the words that she did to Mary. But the Holy Spirit wasn't starting from scratch! The Spirit was building on the character that Elizabeth already possessed, and perhaps just as importantly, on the relationship that Mary and Elizabeth already had. Elizabeth's words of blessing moved Mary to break out into a song of praise—which is contained in that famous passage that has traditionally been called the Magnificat and begins, "My soul magnifies the Lord, and my spirit rejoices in God my Savior" (Luke 1:46-47). Then, immediately after Mary's song, there is a line of Scripture that is often overlooked. It says, "And Mary remained with her about three months and returned to her home." It is a subtle, understated sentence. It finishes the story of Elizabeth and Mary's encounter. Yet it also says everything about the relationship that they had. Elizabeth took Mary under her wing, and Mary spent those uncertain first few months of her pregnancy in Elizabeth's care. Can we really doubt how crucial this time was for Mary? Because she had a mentor that she could look to and learn from, Mary could rest with the assurance that she would be okay.

~

We journey closer and closer to see Jesus when we walk the way of discipleship. That comes through Bible study, prayer, and worship. It also comes through outreach in our communities and mission work. Yet none of those things will ever be effective in our lives without deep and loving relationships with other followers of Jesus. We especially need strong mentors who can show us the way forward in our lives because they have the wisdom and experience of having traveled that road longer than we have, just like Elizabeth was for Mary. We were actually never meant to do discipleship on our own—Jesus himself shows us that when he calls the disciples together as a group. And even when he sends them out, he does so two-by-two.

So much of what we see in our culture today attempts to segregate us into age groups. We get marketing messages for products aimed at Boomers, at Gen Xers, or at Millennials. In a way, it seems as if the messages that media bombard us with are aimed at pitting age groups against one another. And as has been the case since the 1960s in American culture, there is of course always a thinly veiled suggestion that the young should not trust the old and that older generations are out of touch and hopelessly behind the times.

The story of Elizabeth and Mary runs counter to all of that. In their bond, we see an intergenerational relationship that suggests that different age groups very much belong together. And in Mary's willingness to go to Elizabeth in her hour of need, we see an example of a young person trusting her older counterpart exactly for the wisdom and life experience that she has to offer. That isn't an image that would sell a lot of products in contemporary America, but it is exactly the kind of message that the Bible offers time and time again. How much healthier would our churches be if they took their cues from that, rather than from the culture? What if we stopped trying to mimic secular examples in the hopes of competing with contemporary culture and instead just stuck to the wisdom that the Scriptures have been offering us since they were first recorded?

When John Wesley was leading the early Methodist movement in the 1740s, he discovered that, for real and lasting growth in grace to happen, men and women had to be brought together into close relationships where they could "watch over one another in love." That was the phrase Wesley himself used to describe what happened in the class meeting, which was the original small group that the early Methodists employed to help them grow as disciples of Jesus Christ. As we watch from the walls this Advent, waiting for the arrival of our king, we should never do so alone. We should be watching and waiting together. If we are young and new to the faith, we should watch with older mentors who can show us the way of faithfulness. And if we are older and more mature, we should look out for those who are not taking up the role of mentor and guide, just as we were once mentored and guided by those who first raised us up. By doing that, we can stand arm in arm, and side by side, watching for arrival of the One who is our Savior and Lord.

DISCUSSION GUIDE

Prayer:

Lord Jesus Christ, you call us to love God and one another. Come into our hearts this week and remake them by your grace. Fill us with the fullness of your love, so that our lives may be transformed and we can may reach out to those around us as you would have us to do. Stir up within us the desire to form real and lasting relationships with other believers, so that we might experience a greater growth in spiritual maturity each and every day. Amen.

Questions for discussion:

1. The Bible tells us that Zechariah and Elizabeth were good people, yet for many years they were left without their hearts' greatest desire for a child of their own. Have you ever gone for long periods of time in your life feeling like God was not answering your prayers? What was that like?

2. Have you ever gone to a friend or relative that you trust in a time of great need because you knew that the other person would know just what to say to you to make it better? How did you get the point where that was "your person" to turn to when you needed somebody? What is that person's role in your life now?

3. Are you a mentor for someone right now? What is that relationship like? How could you use the wisdom and experience you have gained in your life to help others?

4. Are you watching?

NOTES

[1] R. Alan Culpepper, *The Gospel of Luke*, in Volume IX of *The New Interpreter's Bible* (Nashville: Abingdon Press, 1995), 45.

Chapter Five

The Shepherds' Invitation

Luke 2:1-20

We have watched from the walls as the story of the birth of Jesus has unfolded. Woven throughout that story, we've seen angels at work: telling Zechariah that his wife Elizabeth would give birth to John the Baptist, announcing to Mary that she would bear the Savior of the world, and appearing to Joseph in a dream so that he'd understand that Mary's child was from the Holy Spirit. Yet the angels' work isn't finished once Jesus is born. Just as they had done the work of preparation before Jesus' birth, so too do they have a job to accomplish after it has happened. Angels are God's heralds—they carry important messages and deliver them to where they need to be heard. Since the message of Jesus' birth into the world is the most important piece of news that has ever happened, it needs to be announced! People need to know and bear witness to what God has done.

What is so surprising about what happens next is exactly who it is that the Father sends the angels to visit. He could have sent them to King Herod, so that the ruler of the Jews would know that the Messiah had come. Or, if he wanted a more impressive political figure, he could have sent the angels all the way to Rome to tell Caesar Augustus that the Christ had been born. If he was more interested in letting the religious authorities know, he could have directed an angelic host to descend upon the Temple or even to visit the high priest in his home. But God didn't send the angels to any of those people.

Who did he send them to? He sent them to visit a simple band of shepherds, "out in the field, keeping watch over their flock by night" (Luke 2:8).

The story goes like this: On the very night that Jesus was born, after he had uttered his first cries and his mother Mary had wrapped him in swaddling clothes and laid him in the manger, the Lord sent an angel into the fields outside of the village of Bethlehem where there were shepherds watching their sheep. When the angel appeared, the brightness of God's glory shone around the shepherds and they were afraid. The angel told them not to fear (as so often happens whenever angels appear to people unawares!). Then he said to them, "Behold, I bring you good news of great joy that will be for all the people. For unto you is born this day in the city of David a Savior, who is Christ the Lord" (Luke 2:10-11). The angel then told them where to find the baby Jesus, and with that an entire choir of angels appeared alongside the first and began singing praises to God saying, "Glory to God in the highest, and on earth peace among those with whom he is pleased!" (Luke 2:14).

You have to imagine that the shepherds were practically dumbfounded. Yet the Scripture says that, by the time the angels had left, their fear had dissipated and excitement had taken over. Let's get into town, they said to one another, we've got to see this thing that has happened with our own eyes! So they went ("with haste," the Scripture says) and they found Mary, and Joseph, and the baby Jesus just as the angels had described. Then they shared with Mary and Joseph what the angels had said to them. And on their way out of town, they shared the news with anyone else who would listen! Finally, they went back out to their flocks "glorifying and praising God for all they had heard and seen, as it had been told them" (Luke 2:20).

~

God's decision to send the angelic invitation to the shepherds had a reason behind it—it indicated who Jesus himself was going to be sent to when he entered into his public ministry. Shepherds were rough customers. They weren't exactly in the upper echelons of ancient Jewish society. They were dirty, smelly, and uncouth. They spent their lives out of doors, sleeping under the stars with livestock. The fact that they spent their time with animals out in the fields rather than people put them—quite literally—on the outskirts of their communities. They weren't, in other words, the kind of people you would put at the top of your invitation list when throwing a party.

Then again, the Jesus whose birth the shepherds were called to witness would prove to be a Messiah who came to preach good news to the poor and outcast. He was one who very much believed that the invitation list should include "the poor, the crippled, the lame, and the blind" (Luke 14:13). He was one whose own teaching to his followers would focus on the calling to feed the hungry, clothe the naked, welcome the stranger, and visit the sick and imprisoned (Matthew 25:34-40). So it is fitting that the angel was sent not to princes and potentates, but rather to lowly shepherds keeping watch over their flocks by night. God was honoring the shepherds by choosing them as the first witnesses of Jesus' birth, but he was doing more than that— he was giving a hint from that very first night about what kind of mission Jesus would pursue when the time came for his kingdom-building work to begin.

One of my very favorite possessions is an old Nativity set that I inherited from my grandparents, Boo and Pop. It is handmade, mostly out of cork and plywood. Someone many years ago put it together and painstakingly added individual pieces of grass and straw to give it a realistic look. Then the figurines were added: Joseph and Mary are kneeling with their hands over their hearts. The baby Jesus is lying in a manger with his hands lifted up in an attitude of praise. The scene is framed by a sheep and a cow, resting placidly next to the holy family. And behind them all, standing with a lamb lying across his shoulders, is a young shepherd. He's looking down on the Christ child and doing what the angel called him to do—witnessing the birth of the One who is Savior and Lord.

Photo by the author

I treasure that little Nativity set. When I was a child, it sat on a coffee table in my grandparents' living room during each season of Advent. I remember getting down close to it and studying the little figurines that made up the gentle scene. It was handed down to me when Boo and Pop died, and I've used it every Advent since. It's a simple scene: just the holy family, the animals, and that one lone shepherd. But the shepherd standing there is a reminder to me that the shepherds were there first—before the Wise Men arrived, and long before any crowds gathered to see and hear Jesus preach. They are unnamed, and otherwise unknown. Yet they had a part to play in the Advent story, just as we have a part to play as well. They were the very first watchmen on the walls, and they kept their watch by heeding the angel's call to go into Bethlehem and see where the Christ child lay.

~

When we dig more deeply into the biblical narrative, we find that the image of the shepherd has meaning on many levels. It is true that shepherds represent the lower rungs of society and serve as an indication of who Jesus came to save. It is also true, though, that the image of the shepherd could have royal connotations. After all, Israel's greatest king had started out his career as a shepherd boy. When David first rose to prominence through his fight with Goliath, he did so as a shepherd who was only visiting the Israelite army to carry food to his older brothers. Indeed, the sling and stone that he used to defeat Goliath was a shepherd's weapon! When God called him to succeed Saul as king over Israel, he was simply calling him to act as a shepherd in a different way—to move from shepherding flocks of sheep to shepherding a nation of people. Psalm 78 speaks about how God moved David from one form of shepherding to another:

> He chose David his servant
>> and took him from the sheepfolds;
> from following the nursing ewes he brought him
>> to shepherd Jacob his people,
>> Israel his inheritance.
> With upright heart he shepherded them
>> and guided them with his skillful hand.
>> -Psalm 78:70-72

Through the example of David, we see that the purpose of a king is meant to be to guard and guide his people the same way a shepherd guards and guides his flock. His calling is a calling to lead and protect—to make sure that the flock is tended with care and that the wolves in the tree line are faced down.

We have already seen how Jesus stands in King David's line, so it shouldn't surprise us that David's role as the shepherd of Israel is one that is applied to Jesus himself. The baby who the shepherds came to see on the night of his birth would grow up to be the shepherd of God's people. Jesus is the "great shepherd of the sheep" (Hebrews 13:20) and the "shepherd and guardian of your souls" (1 Peter 2:25, NRSV). He tells us this himself: "I am the good shepherd," Jesus says in John 10:14-15, "I know my own and my own know me, just as the Father knows me and I know the Father. I lay down my life for the sheep." And when he was criticized by the scribes and Pharisees for eating with sinners, Jesus told a parable about a shepherd leaving a flock of 99 sheep to seek out one that was lost (Luke 15:3-7). That shepherd is, of course, Jesus himself. After the repentance and conversion of the tax collector Zaccheus, Jesus rejoiced and then proclaimed, "For the Son of Man came to seek out and to save the lost" (Luke 19:10).

Ultimately, the image of the shepherd is an image for how God wants to relate to us. The shepherds in the Advent story remind us of that. When God spoke through the prophet Ezekiel, he criticized the leaders of Israel for not doing their job as shepherds over the people. God condemned those leaders for their dereliction of duty, saying, "My sheep have become a prey, and my sheep have become food for all the wild beasts" (Ezekiel 34:8). But that is not how God will shepherd us. As Ezekiel tells us,

> For thus says the Lord God: Behold, I myself will search for my sheep and will seek them out. As a shepherd seeks out his flock when he is among his sheep that have been scattered, so will I seek out my sheep, and I will rescue them from all places where they have been scattered on a day of clouds and thick darkness. And I will bring them out from the peoples and gather them from the countries and will bring them into their own land ... I will seek the lost, and I will bring back the strayed, and I will bind up the injured, and I will strengthen the weak... (Ezekiel 34:11-13a,16a).

And of course, it was David himself, the shepherd boy who became a king, who wrote the most memorable words about God being our shepherd in the 23rd psalm: "The Lord is my shepherd; I shall not want. He makes me lie down in green pastures. He leads me beside still waters. He restores my soul" (vv.1-3a, NRSV). When we see the shepherds appear on the night of Jesus' birth, it's as if God is telling us that the true shepherd king has finally come, in the person of Jesus, to gather us into his flock forever.

~

Through the announcement of the angels, the birth of Jesus ceases to be a private affair. They draw the shepherds from watching over their flocks to watching over the manger with Mary and Joseph. In the process, they invite us in too. We have been watching from the walls—through the stories of Mary, Joseph, and Elizabeth. Now the birth of the Christ child has finally happened. Jesus is here! And God doesn't want us to stay at a distance. He wants to draw us close, just as he drew the shepherds. He wants us to know his Son. He wants to pull us in, so that we will know what it means that he has sent us a Good Shepherd. He wants us to know that, because of that babe in the manger, we never have to be lost again. We may sometimes feel like the shepherds—tired, dirty, and living on the margins. But God's desire is that we would be filled with joy. He wants us to know Jesus so that we can have the certainty in our lives that his transforming love is meant for *us*.

DISCUSSION GUIDE

Prayer:

God of the poor and outcast, you come to us no matter who we are or where we have been. Thank you for the mercy and compassion you offer us. Let us always treat one another with that same mercy and compassion in our own lives. Move us to reach out to the least, the last, and the lost. Help us to follow Jesus with everything we have, and give us the guidance of the Holy Spirit. Amen.

Questions for discussion:

1. Read the parable of the lost sheep in Luke 15:3-7. What does this parable mean to you? How is Jesus like the shepherd in the parable?

2. Jesus came to bring good news to the poor, proclaim freedom for the captives, and recovery of sight for the blind. If we are called to follow Jesus, then what does that mean about the church's responsibility to be in ministry with the poor, the hurting, and the forgotten?

3. Have you ever felt like one of the shepherds? What does it mean to you that God would send his angels to such simple, unimportant people and give them the blessing of being the first witnesses to the birth of Jesus Christ?

4. Are you watching?

Chapter Six
The Wise Men's Journey

Matthew 2:1-12

On that cold night when a young woman labored to bring forth her baby into the world, and a worried father did everything he could to make her comfortable amidst the musty surroundings of a stable, God put a star in the sky to summon forth a small group of strangers. Their mission was to witness to the fact the baby who was about to be born was the King of the Jews. The strangers were not Jews themselves. They were from the "East," though exactly what that means we cannot be sure. Many people have suspected that they were from Persia, and that their study of the heavens indicates that they were astrologers. Soon after they saw the new star in the night sky, they set out for Judea so that they could see the newborn child.

We call them the Wise Men.

~

There are three "thrones" in the New Testament, and Jesus reigns from each one of them. These thrones are the three distinct seats of power that he occupies at different points in time. The throne where Jesus ends up (and where he reigns even now) is an actual throne—the throne of heaven. The Bible tells us that "Christ Jesus ... is at the right hand of God and is also interceding for us" (Romans 8:34). It is from that royal seat that he will bring all things to completion at the end of days. As Revelation 21:5 says, "And he who was seated on the throne said, 'Behold, I am making all things new!'" God the Father has granted Jesus the place of honor at "the right hand of the Majesty in heaven" (Hebrews 1:3) because he is Lord of Heaven and earth. All things are under his dominion.

Before Jesus could assume his place on the throne of heaven, though, he first had to reign from his earthly throne. That earthly throne of Jesus was the cross—ironic, because no one understood it as a throne at all while he was on it. Indeed, it was partially through their lack of understanding that the royal status of the cross was publicly shown: the soldiers of Pontius Pilate "clothed him in a purple cloak, twisting together a crown of thorns, they put it on him. And they began to salute him, 'Hail, King of the Jews!'" (Mark 15:17-18). When they had nailed him to the cross, they placed an inscription above his head that read, "The King of the Jews." Yet what they meant as a humiliation was, in reality, an affirmation of who Jesus really was. It was by his own sacrificial death that Jesus defeated the demonic forces of sin and evil that had been attacking God's children since time immemorial. The Apostle Paul shows us this when he says, "And you, who were dead in your trespasses and the uncircumcision of your flesh, God made alive together with him, having forgiven us all our trespasses, by canceling the record of debt that stood against us with its legal demands. This he set aside, nailing it to the cross. He disarmed the rulers and authorities and put them to open shame, by triumphing over them in him" (Colossians 2:13-15). The cross, meant to be an instrument of shame and suffering, was transformed by Jesus into a throne of forgiveness and grace. It was the royal seat to which all of his earthly ministry led.

Yet before he sat on the throne of heaven, and before he mounted the throne of the cross, there was another throne that Jesus held. His very first throne was the manger that his mother Mary laid him in on the night he was born: "And she gave birth to her firstborn son and wrapped him in swaddling clothes and laid him in a manger, because there was no place for them in the inn" (Luke 2:7). Everything about the setting that Joseph, Mary, and Jesus were in says something about the type of king that Jesus would be. His palace was a stable, his royal attendants a motley collection of barnyard animals, and his throne a feeding trough. That, of course, is only fitting for one who was called to preach good news to the poor, who healed the sick and made the blind to see, who forgave sins, and who raised the dead. When this king finally entered his royal city of Jerusalem at the end of his life, he came not riding a great stallion or a gilded chariot, but rather on the back of a donkey. He welcomed little children, and he ate with sinners. He came preaching peace, and his mission was to set the captives free.

The Wise Men weren't the first ones to witness the birth of the Christ child, but they were the ones to show us that the baby Jesus in the manger was nothing less than a king upon his throne. When they arrived in Judea, they went to King Herod and asked, "Where is he who has been born king of the Jews?" (Matthew 2:2). It wasn't a welcome question for Herod—he was, after all, pretty sure that he was the king of the Jews. But Herod wasn't the kind of king they were looking for. They found the king they were looking for in the little village of Bethlehem, the same place about which God had said through Micah the prophet, "But you, O Bethlehem Ephrathah, who are too little to be among the clans of Judah, from you shall come forth for me one who is to be ruler in Israel, whose coming forth is from of old, from ancient days" (Micah 5:2). The star guided them there, and it eventually led them to the place where the holy family was staying:

> When they saw the star, they rejoiced exceedingly with great joy. And going into the house they saw the child with Mary his mother, and they fell down and worshiped him. Then, opening their treasures, they offered him gifts, gold and frankincense and myrrh (Matthew 2:10-11).

They fell down before him and offered him gifts fit for a king because he *is* a king. He is the king of all creation, and in the form of a babe seated upon his manger-throne he had come at last into his kingdom.

~

The Wise Men are one of those wonderful, mysterious parts of the Advent story. They emerge from somewhere distant —"the East" is all we know. And it is not even clear what to call them. We use the term "Wise Men" because that is how the original Greek *magoi* was rendered in the King James Version of the Bible back in 1611. Some translations call them magi and some call them astrologers. There is a tradition that they were kings, which is based off of the idea that Isaiah 60:3 is a prophecy for their arrival: "And nations shall come to your light, and kings to the brightness of your rising."

Yet there is nothing in the Bible itself to prove that they are kings, and the idea that they are wise men or sages is just a guess given that they tell Herod they observed a star in the heavens that called them westward. It never even says that there were three of them—that idea simply comes from the fact that they brought three gifts of gold, frankincense, and myrrh. The Gospel of Matthew also never specifically says that the men are Gentiles, although their faraway origin and their practice of astrology seems to suggest that this must be the case.

If they are Gentiles, then their presence before Jesus is something like the Gentile equivalent of the visit of the Jewish shepherds on the night of Jesus' birth. We see in that something of a foreshadowing of the church itself. Just like the (Jewish) shepherds from around Bethlehem were called to witness to the birth of Jesus first, so too would the church begin with faithful Jews recognizing Jesus as Christ and Lord. Yet just as Jesus would later command his followers to go into the world and make disciples of all nations at the end of Matthew's gospel, the (Gentile) Wise Men represent the very first of those nations to bow down before the Messiah. It's for this reason that John Wesley referred to the Wise Men as the "first fruits of the Gentiles."[1] They give the first fulfillment of a prophecy not even yet uttered at the time of their arrival in Bethlehem: that there will come a day when, "every knee should bow... and every tongue confess that Jesus Christ is Lord, to the glory of God the Father" (Philippians 2:10-11).

So what we see in the arrival of the Wise Men is nothing less than a sign of God's universal mercy and love! Gentile Christian believers have long taken great comfort in the knowledge of God's word through the prophet Isaiah that shows us God's redeeming love going out to all the nations:

Fear not, for I am with you;
> I will bring your offspring from the east,
> and from the west I will gather you.
I will say to the north, Give up,
> and to the south, Do not withhold;

> bring my sons from afar
>> and my daughters from the end of the earth,
> everyone who is called by my name,
>> whom I created for my glory,
>> whom I formed and made.

-Isaiah 43:5-7

The God who called Israel to be his chosen people has sent a Savior for the people of the whole world. Like a wild olive shoot, he has grafted the church onto the tree of Israel. And regardless of whether one is Jew or Gentile, the good news tells us that "if you confess with your mouth that Jesus is Lord and believe in your heart that God raised him from the dead, you will be saved" (Romans 10:9).

The doctrine of universal atonement tells us that Jesus Christ died for the sins of the whole world. It comes from the Scriptural teaching that "God did not send his Son into the world to condemn the world, but in order that the world might be saved through him" (John 3:17). This is unbelievably wonderful news for us! And the first inkling that we have of it in the life of Jesus is the moment that those three strange men from the East arrive at the doorstep of Joseph and Mary so that they can present gifts fit for a king to their infant son.

~

My favorite image of the Wise Men comes from the paintbrush of a French artist named James Tissot. He was a popular painter of upper-class men and women in France and England in the late 19th century. Yet in the 1880s, he journeyed to the holy land with a desire to renew his faith and learn about the actual physical places where the people of the Bible lived and walked. The result was a series of watercolor paintings about both Old and New Testament stories that are simply remarkable. One of those is a depiction of the Wise Men as they journey towards Bethlehem and the Christ child.

James Tissot's painting bears little resemblance to the sentimentalized versions of the Wise Men from so much popular Christian art. Tissot depicts them as riding on the backs of camels at the head of a caravan through a lonely and rugged valley. Their faces are drawn and their posture is wary. Two of the three carry spears in addition to their riding crops, hinting at a journey not only long but also dangerous. Everything about the painting suggests that the three men's path from their faraway home in the East to the village of Bethlehem in Judea is not an easy one. Yet something compels them to keep going, to press ahead through long miles of waterless desert, to keep striving towards their goal despite the dangers of bandits and wild animals, to keep following the star until it shows them where the King of the Jews has been born.

These three men who bear their gifts of gold, frankincense, and myrrh, will be the first Gentiles to recognize who Jesus really is. And in that sense, they foreshadow the future revelation that Jesus Christ would be not only Savior to the Jews but also Savior of the whole world. Long before God moved Peter to recognize that the Gentiles, too, had received the Holy Spirit, and long before the Lord showed to Paul that he was to be the Apostle to the Gentiles, God drew these first three Gentiles to worship the Christ child in Bethlehem. It is perhaps in the actual journey they had to make to see Jesus that we can understand something of the spiritual journey that each of us makes as we seek to know him as well. For us, the journey can be long and hard. We know what it means to travel through spiritual deserts where the nourishing waters we need are scarce to be found. And we can often relate to the sense that we are being called to travel to a place where we've never been before—and to a destination that can seem so distant we don't know if we'll ever get there.

Yet God calls out to us, just as surely as he put that star in the eastern sky. He draws us to his Son. And he wants us to bring precious gifts, gifts that are even more valuable than gold and frankincense and myrrh. He wants us to bring the gift of ourselves, to offer our hearts and lives before the throne of our Savior Jesus.

~

Of all the people in the Advent story, it might be the Wise Men with whom we can most closely identify. All of us, in a sense, begin in a faraway country. We yearn for a sense of belonging, and we want to believe that there is a deeper purpose for our lives. When we can get away from the lights of our cities and the glow of our screens, we look up to the heavens and wonder where, in all that great starry firmament, there is an answer to the hard and perplexing questions we face throughout our lives.

God knows our need, and He reaches out to beckon us to Him. "Thou hast made us for Thyself," as Saint Augustine wrote, "And our hearts are restless until they rest in Thee." As the star shone in the East calling the Magi to Bethlehem, so does the Father's light shine in the darkness of our spiritual night and call us to come to know his Son, the Lord Jesus.

So we come, making our way over a spiritual journey that can take us through dry and desolate lands. We might be tempted to stop and inquire in a grand city where those with title and position will be all too happy to give us their own advice. But the journey is not over until we have gone all the way—through the desert, past the glittering capital and on to the humble little village where He waits for us. His kingship does not conform to the ways of the world. His throne is a feeding trough, his attendants are barn animals, and his palace is a stable. His only army is a band of lowly shepherds, yet angels sing for Him. When we come into his presence, the purity and power of His love are overwhelming. Then, in a moment too profoundly beautiful to describe in words, we realize that He bears that love for us. And so we fall to our knees, open our arms, and give him all we have. The Wise Men may have been the first Gentiles to bow down to Jesus, but they set a pattern that countless Gentiles have followed since—all of whom recognize that the one born King of the Jews is both Christ and Lord.

DISCUSSION GUIDE

Prayer:

Dearest Lord Jesus, thank you for coming to us in the flesh to be our Savior. You sacrificed everything so that we could know eternal life. By your grace, make us holy in heart and life. Draw us close to yourself, and never let us go. Forgive us of the guilt of our sins, and free us from the power of sin so that we can live fully for you. Be our Lord and God, and let us walk by the light of your love. We lay our lives before you. Amen.

Questions for discussion:

1. What do you think the Wise Men believed they were doing when they followed the star from the East? What do you think the hardest part of their journey would have been?

2. How did you come to know the Lord Jesus? Did you have to travel over difficult terrain, through a dry and desolate land, with dangers all around? What kept you going?

3. The Wise Men offered Jesus gifts of gold, frankincense, and myrrh. What can you offer to Jesus? What do you think he wants from you?

4. Are you watching?

NOTES

[1] John Wesley, Note on Matthew 2:1, in *John Wesley's Commentary on the Bible*, ed. G. Roger Schoenhals (Grand Rapids, MI: Francis Asbury Press, 1990).

[2] This anticipation is suggested by Douglas R.A. Hare, *Matthew* (Louisville: John Knox Press, 1993), 13.

Conclusion
Watching For The Return Of The King

There was once a bishop of the city of Carthage named Cyprian who happened to live at one of the most difficult times in the history of the church. He lived from about A.D. 200 to 258, and he was the leader of the church in Carthage during a series of severe persecutions by Roman emperors who wanted to destroy the Christian faith. Much of Cyprian's time as bishop was spent trying to hold the church together and deal with the difficult issue of what to do about Christians who renounced their faith in order to escape torture or death at the hands of the Romans. One of the tendencies of Christians throughout history has been that, when the times they are living in get particularly hard, the hope and expectation of the return of Jesus Christ burns brighter. That was the case for Cyprian, and the hope he had for Jesus' return shines through in his writing. He even puts that hope in the language of watching. In an important essay from his time as bishop where he was arguing for the unity of the church in the face of schism and persecution, Cyprian writes:

> Let us await the sudden advent of the Lord with ever-watchful care, that when he knocks our faith may be found awake to receive of him the reward of vigilance ... As watchful servants, we shall reign with Christ in his kingdom.[1]

What we do during the season of Advent looks both to the past and to the future. It is about memory on the one hand, and hope on the other. We remember and celebrate the coming of Jesus Christ into the world, born to the Virgin Mary in that little stable in Bethlehem. And we also look forward to his promised return, when his kingdom shall come in its fullness and we will rejoice with angels and archangels and all the company of heaven as he remakes this world and welcomes us into the New Jerusalem.

Cyprian's counsel to us is to remember that our watching counts. It matters that we remain faithful and vigilant, looking forward to that day when the trump shall sound and the Lord shall descend to bring all things to completion. Colossians 4:2 tells us, "Continue steadfastly in prayer, being watchful in it with thanksgiving." That theme of watchfulness runs throughout the Scriptures—we are called to keep awake, to make sure our wicks are trimmed, and to be ready. When we celebrate Advent each year, we are practicing that readiness.

We are the watchmen on the walls, and as we retell and relive the story of Jesus' birth, we prepare ourselves for his return at the end of days. As we do that, it is always important for us to remember that we do not do it passively. God calls us to gather close, with Mary and Joseph around the manger. The shepherds are on our right and the Wise Men on our left. We look down with awe upon the Christ child who lays there as proof that God loves us so much that he comes to us in human form. And come again he will.

Are you watching?

NOTES

1 Cyprian of Carthage, *The Unity of the Catholic Church*, ¶27, in *Early Latin Theology*, ed. S.L. Greenslade (Louisville: Westminster John Knox Press, 1956), 141-142.

About the Author

Andrew C. Thompson is the senior pastor of First United Methodist Church in Springdale, Arkansas. He holds the Doctor of Theology degree from Duke University Divinity School (Durham, NC), and prior to taking his appointment in Springdale he spent four years on the faculty of Memphis Theological Seminary (Memphis, TN). His most recent book is *The Means of Grace: Traditioned Practice in Today's World* (Seedbed).

At First Church Springdale, Andrew's ministry emphasis is centered around preaching, teaching, staff & congregational leadership, and missions. Over the past few years, he and his pastoral team have led the church in developing a three-fold disciple-making paradigm of gathering in worship, growing in spiritual maturity, and going forth into the world in mission. This "gather/grow/go" paradigm reflects the biblical model for discipleship formation present both in the four gospels and the Acts of the Apostles.

Andrew and his wife Emily have three wonderful children that keep them busy. Together they enjoy the natural and cultural attractions of life in the Ozark Mountains of Northwest Arkansas.

Chapter 1 Notes

Chapter 2 Notes

Chapter 3 Notes

Chapter 4 Notes

Chapter 5 Notes

Chapter 6 Notes

Made in the USA
Middletown, DE
26 August 2020